Put Down the Book
and DO something!

Roger Webb

Copyright © 2017 Roger Webb

All rights reserved.

ISBN-10: 0692722122
ISBN-13: 978-0692722121

DEDICATION

To my kids - Angel, Princess, Skipper, Jack, and J Dawg... You are the reason for everything I do! I love you to the moon and back to infinity! You inspire me daily and are my greatest teachers in life! May you live a life that will create generations of love, peace, intimacy, and an intense connection to humanity!
Live big and dream bigger!

CONTENTS

1	Introduction	Pg 1
2	How to Use This Book	Pg 6
3	The Voices in Your Head!	Pg 8
4	Understanding the Subconscious Mind	Pg 12
5	The Anatomy of Limiting Beliefs	Pg 15
6	I Am	Pg 25
7	The Prices we Pay	Pg 33
8	Getting to the Root	Pg 41
9	Re-framing Perceptions	Pg 55
10	Building Massive Evidence	Pg 68
11	Loving Yourself Unconditionally	Pg 77
12	Living Consciously	Pg 79
13	Who are you & What do You Really Want?	Pg 83
14	90 Days of Breakthrough	Pg 91
16	The Dandelion	Pg 159

ACKNOWLEDGMENTS

The biggest thanks goes to my kids. Wanting to be the best dad I could be, is what put me on the path of personal development. Without your inspiration, I can't even begin to imagine where I'd be... Or more accurately, where I wouldn't be! I love you forever!

I had many mentors and teachers along the way, but I need to offer a very special thank you to one man who took me under his wing, and taught me to feel love and live life in a way I didn't know possible - Dr. David G. Lunt, thank you for teaching me how to live from my heart. Thank you for teaching me the importance of laughing from my soul. Many generations will be different because of your love and example!

There are so many others who have helped to mold me into the man that I am today. You have taught me to lead, and to love. You have shown me tough love when I needed it, and offered me immense support in every area of my life. To each of you, you know what role you have played in my development, and I thank you.

To Savanna. Eternal gratitude for your friendship & love.
Every life with you has been a treasure. Until the next time...

To God...
Your are in me, and I am in you. That Divine Truth changed me forever, and allowed me to trust, for the first time in my life. I am simply shining a light for others to find the path that is right for them.
Thank you for allowing me to see and know this gift!

1 - INTRODUCTION

I'm often asked as a coach, what books I recommend. This is a tough question for me, and one I really don't like being asked! There are thousands of amazing books out there on personal development. I've never read one that I would classify as a "bad book," and every person has unique needs and interests depending on where they are in their life at that moment. I have a unique view on personal development books. One of my very first mentors, over 20 years ago, challenged me to live a life where I didn't depend on what he called "SHELF help books," but rather, focus my life on DOING, LIVING, BEING a person of growth. learning, and discovery - every day.

With this advice in mind, I have had amazing experiences almost daily that have beat me down, supported me, taught me, and boosted me up. I am not, in any way discouraging you from reading amazing books! I am simply challenging you to take daily action on the things you learn in the books you are reading. I am nearing completion of my second book, "PUT THE BOOK DOWN and DO something!"

Years ago, I was on a flight, and I read an article in a paper that my seatmate had finished. It cited a study that supported this thinking, and shaped how I ran my workshops and retreats from then on. I don't remember who conducted the study, or what the reasoning was, but the results were profound.

This study followed the personal growth and development of a group of people who self identified as moderately interested in personal development. They divided the group into three different and distinct sub groups. Each group was given a different format for their development over the period of a year. The first group were allowed to read self-help books, as many as they wanted. They weren't allowed any other form of development. Group 2 was sent to personal development lectures, and group 3 participated in workshops, retreats, and more experiential type of training environments.

They were looking to discover if any method of learning/training was more effective than any other. What they found, was fairly profound to me. They went to the group who read the books, thirty days after the completion of the study, and it was reported that less than 10% of them had significant change in their lives. Sixty days later, they surveyed the group who sat through the lectures. 20% of them reported significant change in their lives and circumstances. They surveyed group 3 six months later. Remember, this was the group who took part in the retreats and workshops. What they found, was that 80% of them had remarkable, positive change in their lives... Even after 6 months!

It is my firm belief, from the results of this study as well as my own experience, with clients, and my own personal development journey, that TRUE and LASTING change comes much more with experiential, active, hands on training. I know from my NLP training, that the more senses you engage in an activity, the stronger your subconscious connections will be. When you are actively involved in this type of work, you will have much longer lasting and permanent results.

I am not a opponent to reading. I love great books. The problem comes when those books cease to be SELF help books, and they transform into SHELF help books, because you read them and set them back on the shelf to collect dust.

I am here to lead you on a journey. I am here to hold a light for you as you journey along the path of personal development. I am here to give you the tools to get to know your limiting beliefs in a very intimate way. When you are able to know them, you will be able to overcome them!

This book is meant to be discovered. It's meant to empower you. It's meant as a teacher. Read it, devour it, and then DO SOMETHING! Use the activities outlined to dismantle your limiting beliefs one brick at a time! It's about TAKING ACTION! It's about DOING!

When I began coaching, I discovered that most people long to live lives that are bigger, better, greater, happier, more successful, and wealthier than they are currently experiencing. I also discovered that the same people who have these great aspirations, also have "programming" that often defeats them, long before they even get out of the starting gate. I began to turn the focus in my practice to these limiting beliefs that sabotage our greatness! I became obsessed with learning all that I could about this phenomena. Where do these beliefs come from? Why do we have them? Why does it seem so difficult for many to overcome them?

I am a spiritual man. Regardless of how you define your spirituality, I have found that most people can identify with the belief that we are inherently good, amazing, powerful, Divine beings. We start this life out with everything that we need to be massively happy and successful. So what stops us? Why aren't we ALL massively happy and successful? Why do some people seem to have an easier time creating that happiness and success in their lives, than others do?

I have had the amazing gift of being mentored by some very powerful teachers, who understand concepts of the mind, of life, and of spirituality. I want to be clear - when I say spirituality, I am not talking about church. I'm not talking about theology. I am talking about the spiritual truths that are present in every major spiritual practice. I call these Universal Truths. I've yet to meet a client who has not found a way to fit what I teach, into their own beliefs, and I challenge you to do the same. They are Universal Truths, regardless of what package they are wrapped up in.

I have spent many years in developing an understanding of how the subconscious mind works. These limiting beliefs we speak of, have taken up residence deep in your subconscious. The tools you will get in this book will serve as their eviction notice.

I invite you to challenge yourself as you experience the journey that this book is meant to put you on. It's a process. A Journey. Meant to be taken one step at a time. I strongly advise you to be gentle with yourself. Many of these limiting beliefs have deep roots in physical, emotional, or even sexual trauma. Go slow. Be mindful of yourself. If you find that tough things come up, or some past darkness from your life is beginning to be exposed, PLEASE do yourself a favor, and seek out the support of someone who is professionally trained to help you through the healing process - a counselor, therapist, coach, etc. I personally recommend finding someone who has been trained in NLP, Timeline Therapy, EMDR, or any other form of subconscious therapy. Please don't let this scare you off! This is amazing, wonderful, beautiful work! I have a DEEP amount of respect for people who are willing to take on their own lives to improve them. Personal growth is not about rainbows, butterflies, and unicorns! Sometimes it's a hard, painful, scary process... But I can promise you that when you continue through the hard parts, you will find greater love, beauty, and magic in your life than you ever dreamed possible!

One of the most important things I can ask of you right now, is that you disregard the lies that you may have been told, about your ability to have an amazing life. I ask you to not buy in to the idea that it's hard or impossible to overcome your limiting beliefs. I have massive amounts of evidence that not only is it possible and probable, it's actually a lot easier than you think!

If you want a bigger, better, greater, happier, or more successful life, I can PROMISE you that if you follow the principles and the steps outlined in this book, you will discover that your own limiting beliefs have less and less power over you. You will wake up one day, look around, and discover that you are indeed living the life of your dreams! When that happens, I invite you to contact me, and tell me of your success!

I am not an English major. This book, as well as about 6 others in my head, got put off for many years, because of the (limiting) belief I had, that I am not a good enough technical writer. As I have done my own work, I have come to a place where I don't really care! I know the influence these principles can have. I know the difference this work can make in your life. I no longer care about how proper my grammar is, or if my spell check misses a word! A belief that only "those people" can write a best selling book, has caused many amazing books to be left unwritten. I'm a normal guy, with a normal middle class education, and I have an amazing gift to share with you that could potentially change your life. I no longer give a damn what those of you reading it with your proofing pen, will think. Instead, I'd invite you to look at what limiting belief you have that is behind your need to find fault in others! (said in the most loving, supportive tone) So here we go...

2 - HOW TO USE THIS BOOK

The first thirteen chapters of this book are meant to be a guide to help lay a foundation for the work you are about to undertake. These first chapters will bring you a greater understanding and knowledge In three main areas. 1. You will explore the subconscious mind, and how it works for you and against you. 2. You will learn about limiting beliefs... Where they come from. How they work, how they sabotage your life, and where their weaknesses are. 3. You will be reminded about the amazing, wonderful. Powerful truths about you.

Once you are armed with that foundation, you will have the tools that you need to begin shaping your life in the direction of your most amazing goals and dreams!

I encourage you to turn this book into a personal handbook. Write in it, highlight it, mark it up! Forget everything your elementary school librarian told you! I hope that when you close the back cover, that this book looks old and worn out!

My hope is that by the time you hit chapter fifteen, that you are ready and prepared to put it all to the test, and blow those limiting beliefs away!

This book is designed to give you a 90 day "program" of breaking through your limiting beliefs. Please don't think that once you are done with the 90 days you are done. I invite you to revisit this experience any time in your life that you feel a need for a tune up.

Chapter fourteen is a guide. It is meant to be used as an experiential journey, an opportunity for you to notice the slow destruction of your limiting beliefs with every turn of the page! Each page begins with a task... A simple challenge, created to address a specific area of your limiting beliefs.

Some of them will make no sense. Some of them will seem silly. Some of them will push your buttons, bring up fears, or just seem plain stupid. I encourage you to trust this process, and take them each very seriously - especially the ones that bring up your fears, push your buttons, or just seem plain stupid. They are often the ones that have the most unexpected impact on your life. (almost always!)

On each page, along with the task, you will find open, lined space, that is there for you to write, journal, and document your experience. I can promise you that if you add the writing piece to this experience, your limiting beliefs will be defeated much faster, and much more permanently. If you need more space to write, I would suggest that you find a small notebook, diary, or journal to use as an overflow.

If you want to elevate your experience even more get a friend, or better yet, a group of friends to do it with you! I can't imagine a more amazing, and life changing book club!

Remember, his isn't your ordinary book! It is specifically designed to support you in CREATING an amazing life, as you TAKE ACTION on overcoming your limiting beliefs! I challenge you to take this experience very seriously. Commit to it. Allow yourself to be fully present and fully engaged!

You might be thinking. "Wow! What did I get myself into?!" Let me answer that question for you. You are about to take a step into the life that you've always dreamed of. You are about to accomplish the things you've attempted a hundred times and failed! You are about to reach levels of success and happiness that you have wished for, for years! Hold on, buckle up, and get ready for an amazing ride!!

3 - THE VOICES IN YOUR HEAD

I invite you to think about something amazing that you'd like to accomplish or create in your life. Maybe it's a new career, or a new hobby. Maybe it's pursuing a new relationship. Maybe you are thinking about an awesome vacation that you'd like to take, or a car you'd like to own. Think about the big stuff! Maybe there are some goals and dreams that you had in the past, that you have given up on. Take a minute and think about those! Think about living in a world where all of that is a reality, and you did it!

Now sit quietly for a minute and listen. What do you "hear" in your mind? Maybe for some of them, you hear positive, excited, supportive thoughts. I'm sure there are some however, where the thought is followed by a, "Yeah, but..."

- Yeah, but... I'm not good enough...
- Yeah, but... I'm not smart enough...
- Yeah, but... I'm not worthy of...
- Yeah, but... I'm not pretty/handsome enough...
- Yeah, but... I'm not healthy enough...
- Yeah, but... I'm ugly...
- Yeah, but... Money is bad...
- Yeah, but... Success makes people bad...
- Yeah, but... I can't...
- Yeah, but... That's for them - not for me...
- Yeah, but... I can't do that anymore...
- Yeah, but... I'm afraid...
- Yeah, but... I don't deserve...
- Yeah, but...
- Yeah, but...
- Yeah, but...

You get the idea? What was your "Yeah, but...?" What are the things that you believe about yourself? What voices have let you from getting what you want in life?

Our Personal Belief System (heretofore referred to as our Personal BS) propels and supports us, and at the same time it defeats us, discourages us, and often keeps us from even trying at all. For most people today, unfortunately our limiting, or negative beliefs have far more power than our positive and supportive ones.

As you use the tools laid out in this book, it is my hope that you will become more and more consciously aware of when these limiting beliefs are showing up. That is 75% of the battle.

Often these limiting beliefs are deeply intertwined with each other. In my own life, for many years, fear ran me. It controlled everything I did, every decision I made, ever risk I took, etc. EVERYTHING was decided in my life, by fear. When I began my own journey of personal development, I became harshly aware of the role that fear played in my life. But I also began to discover that the fear was intertwined by a pretty strong belief that I wasn't worthy or deserving of anything amazing and great. I had great fear, that if I ever did accomplish any of my dreams, that it would end in disaster, which would completely spin me into a vortex of sadness and humiliation. This realization poured fuel on the fire that drove my fear! If I believed that I was so unworthy or incapable, that all of my efforts would end in failure or embarrassment, then why on Earth would I ever even accomplish anything in the first place? I justified that it was much better and safer to live a mediocre life, with no risk, that it was to experience the failure that was certain to come if I attempted anything great. We will discuss later, where these beliefs came from, and you will see how strong they can be!

I also had a very strong belief around love. I was not lovable. That's what I believed. If you ask anyone around me they would laugh at that one! In everyone else's eyes, I was very lovable, and incredibly well loved, but the voices in my head said that I wasn't.

Because of that, I rarely put myself out there to form new friendships. I was a true wallflower (at least in my own mind!)

So, whenever anything came up in my life, that challenged any of these things I believed, there was instant sabotage, and all of those limiting beliefs got to be right.

In chapter 4, we will discuss the subconscious mind in much greater detail, but it is important now, to point out that many, if not all of these beliefs are at such a subconscious level that you may not even be aware that they are even speaking. It's not until later, while looking back, that you may see how much influence they have had over you in your life.

My first challenge for you, is to be very conscious in the next 24 hours of the dialogue in your head. Take notice how often the negative talk about yourself comes up. Notice where those voices stop you! Notice how much impact they have on our day to day life. It's like asking you to be aware of when your lungs take a breath. It's so automatic, that we aren't even aware it's happening!

One of my mentors once asked me a question that rocked my world. "Would you date someone who talks about you, the way that YOU talk about you?" Holy cow!! I hadn't even been that aware of it prior to that conversation. We want to be surrounded by people who uplift and speak nothing but kindness to us... Yet the words we speak to ourselves either out loud, in our heads, or unconsciously, are usually harsh, unsupportive, and sometimes downright mean.

If you have already done some of this work, and you are lucky enough to have a lot of loud supportive, uplifting voices in your head, I challenge you to find the subtle places where your limiting beliefs make themselves known. If you believe that you have no limiting beliefs I would argue that that very statement is a limiting belief. One of the foremost requirements to achieving success with this journey, is honesty. Honesty with yourself. I truly do not believe that there is a person alive who has no limiting beliefs. It's part of the human experience. Find them. Look deep if you have to!

There is a difference between having a positive mental attitude, and having no limiting beliefs. Our limiting beliefs are formed over a lifetime. They are hard wired into our thought processes. I am a HUGE believer of having a positive mental attitude, and we will discuss that later, but it is important to be aware, that even with your positive talk, these limiting beliefs are still trying to make themselves known!

In chapter 5, we will begin taking an actual inventory of your limiting beliefs, but I encourage you now, to begin listening for them. Make note of them as you notice, on page 23. There are some activities later on that you will need to have them identified.

For now, the important thing, is that you are beginning to become aware of them. Notice when they are on your side, and notice when they defeat you. As we will learn in a later chapter, our Personal BS is the filter for all of our amazing inspiration and ideas. The goal here, is to reprogram that filtration process, to always be working on the positive beliefs... Many of which might only be wishes today!

4- UNDERSTANDING THE SUBCONSCIOUS MIND

Before we look too deeply into limiting beliefs, I think it's first important to have a good understanding of the subconscious mind. Hundreds of books have been written about the subconscious, and I'm sure many know much more than I do, but after 20 years of working with the subconscious mind, I have a pretty good understanding of how it works, and there are a few specific aspects of the subconscious that we need to understand, before we dive deeper into limiting beliefs. It's easiest to describe it how I teach children about it.

Take a look at the diagram on the next page. Let's start with the Conscious Mind. We call this "The Boss." "The Boss" is responsible for saying what needs to be done. In life however, "The Boss" isn't always our own voice. It can quite often be the voice of those around us. That kid on the playground who made fun of you every day. That teacher who told you that you weren't smart enough. The coach who told you that you weren't good enough. That ex boyfriend who told you that you were ugly... Get the idea? Any message that is fed into the mind, the conscious mind gives the direction to the Subconscious. The conscious mind takes all the messages received in our lives, and translates them into how we should feel, act, be, etc. Unfortunately, many of those messages, come from less than positive sources. The messages that "The Boss" transmits, are the very things that become our Personal Belief System. Both positive and negative messages we receive, form how we think, feel, and act about our environment or ourselves.

Then we have the Subconscious Mind. Otherwise known as "The Genie." In the original story of Aladdin's Lamp (before the limiting minds of the western world messed it up), the Genie was only allowed to say ONE THING... "Your wish is my command!" Whatever the Genie is asked for, it creates. Our subconscious mind works in a similar way, in regards to the messages that it hears. The messages that it hears the loudest, the most frequent, and with the strongest emotion, are the ones that gets heard. And then "The Genie" goes to work, creating the very thing it is told to create! Remember, "The Genie" is only allowed to say one thing - "Your wish is my command!" It will set actions in motion that will create a life that supports the messages that it receives.

The third level, which we will discuss with a little more in detail later on, is what I refer to as the SuperConscious. Volumes upon volumes of book and scripture have been written about the Superconscious. This part of our consciousness has many names. Some call it God, The Universe, The Great I Am, etc. Whatever name you call it by, it is the part of our consciousness that connects us all, and it's the Source of all ideas, thought, inspiration, etc.

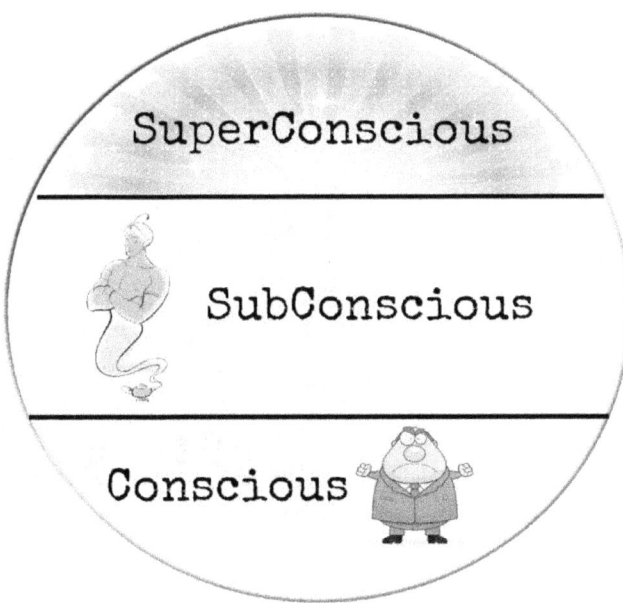

A good demonstration of how these levels of consciousness can play out, is found in India. Elephants are viewed by many as the most physically powerful animals on the planet. When a baby elephant begins it's training, the trainer first places a large chain around it's leg, and fastens the other end to a stake that is immovable. The baby elephant pulls away, and soon realizes that it can't go anywhere. The message that the elephant is receiving from "The Boss," is that it can't run away. It can't go further form the stake than the chain will allow. Every time it feels the tug of the chain, "The Boss" reiterates that message. Over and over and over again. "The Genie," after receiving this same message multiple times, crosses it's arms, blinks it's eyes, and says, "Your wish is my command! We aren't going anywhere!"

After a few weeks with the chain on it's leg, the trainer replaces the chain with a much smaller chain that is clearly not as sturdy as the one before. However, when the elephant feels the tug on it's leg, "The Genie" is reminded that it's not going anywhere! Every few weeks, the chain is reduced, until it is finally replaced with a piece of twine. But each time the elephant feels the tug on it's leg, "The Boss" and "The Genie" do their jobs, exactly how they are supposed to! You and I both know that the elephant could snap that twine with one little twitch, but the elephant believes that there is still a large chain keeping it from going anywhere!

We all have "chains" around our leg, holding us back from going where we want to go. Our chains are called Limiting Beliefs. These beliefs are made up of the messages we received, or told ourselves, so many times, that our Genie convinced us that we couldn't go anywhere. And yet, if we started to truly see and understand the truths about ourselves, we would know that these chains have a much looser hold that we think!

5 - THE ANATOMY OF LIMITING BELIEFS

"If you know the enemy and know yourself, you need not fear the result of a hundred battles. If you know yourself but not the enemy, for every victory gained you will also suffer a defeat. If you know neither the enemy nor yourself, you will succumb in every battle."
— Sun Tzu, The Art of War

Before you can overcome your limiting beliefs, it is important to know where they came from. The better you understand their origins, the more powerful you will become in your desire to overcome them.

I truly believe that if mankind were to stop believing the limiting beliefs in our minds, and started living the lives that we are capable of, we would live in a world greater than any Utopia that has ever been described!

Now that you have a base understanding of our levels of consciousness, and how they affect our beliefs, let's take look at how our limiting beliefs are formed. Limiting Beliefs, are deeply rooted subconscious beliefs that are formed by a lifetime of experiences. Typically, they are rooted in experiences that have a significant amount of emotion connected to them. I'll use an experience from a former client to demonstrate.

Mitch asked me to help him work through issues he had with his father. At 35 years old, he could barely stand be be in the same room as his dad. He said he had felt that way as long as he could remember. We worked together through several subconscious techniques, looking for further insight and understanding of his feelings. Then the breakthrough came. We were doing a closed eye visualization, and he remembered being 4 years old ,standing in the driveway, watching his father drive away. He remembers crying hysterically. He said that he wanted to go with his dad, and the last thing he remembered was his dad yelling at him, saying he couldn't go, and he got in the car and drove away. Sounds simple enough. I'm sure many of us have memories similar to that. But in this small 4 year old mind, without a lifetime of experiences to teach him, there was only one thing that he felt at that moment... "Dad doesn't want me."

As human beings we have a very strong driving force in our behavior... we don't want to be wrong. So to preserve that need, 4 year old Mitch's brain begins looking for evidence to prove that he is right about his perception that "dad doesn't want me." Every time his dad said something just so, or did something that could be interpreted by this young and inexperienced mind, as supporting this new idea, it fed his subconscious fire. It didn't take long before his dad did enough things (that he was totally unaware of) to allow "The Boss" to build a case for the argument that Mitch's dad indeed didn't want him. A belief is now formed. I can imagine what it was like in that home when Mitch was a teenager. Imagine being a child with a (subconscious) belief that his own dad didn't want him! Remember, it is a SUBCONSCIOUS belief which means that Mitch is not aware of it. He just knows there is tension and frustration. His belief then began to shape his behavior and he began acting out and distancing himself from his father. Thirty years later, a man sat in my office with zero positive relationship with his dad, and he was hurting.

Now let's break this down... Young Mitch first had a perception that maybe his dad didn't want him. A perception formed in a very immature mind, that didn't have the experience of life to teach him context. He eventually formed enough evidence (formed by that same immature mind) that his perception was indeed fact. Once a perception is believed, it takes up residency as a part of our Personal Belief System. A great mentor of mine, calls that her Personal B.S.! Our beliefs then shape our behaviors in life and bring about the exact results that we have today. What are your results? If they aren't what you want them to be, I would suggest that your Personal B.S. Needs some spring cleaning!

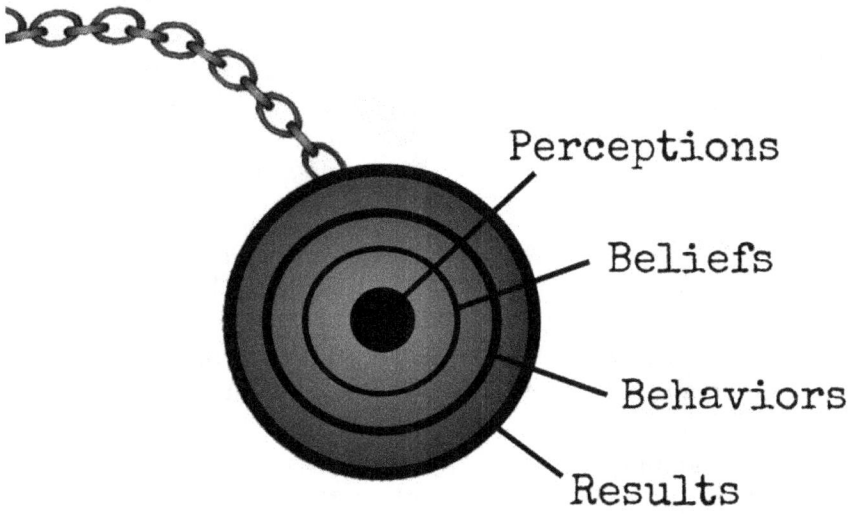

I was able to help Mitch to re-frame those earliest perceptions. As he was able to look at the event through the eyes of a 35 year old man, who brought a lifetime of experiences and context, he was able to see the truth. His dad simply couldn't take him to wherever he was going! He was probably in a hurry, didn't have time to deal with a fussy 4 year old, and got a little cranky. He got in his car, and drove away. Period. He didn't love his son any less. He simply couldn't take him wherever he was going! I wish everyone could see the light that came on in Mitch's eyes as he realized all of this! He looked at me, with tears in his eyes, and said, "So, you mean to tell me that none of what I believed was true? My dad not only wanted me, he loved me? And I was the one who pushed HIM away?" A few weeks later, Mitch went home for Thanksgiving. The first time in years that he had gone. While he was home, he had an amazing conversation with his dad. He told him what he had learned. Today, Mitch and his father are very close, and have spent the last few years rebuilding a great relationship!

Now let's put all of this together and look at how all of this affects us today, in real life. Have you ever had a big goal or dream? Something you wanted really bad? But then it just never seemed to come together? You did all the things you were taught. You followed all the right steps. But it still, for some reason, just didn't come to fruition. Usually, we just chalk it up to "a good attempt," and establish the attitude of, "I'll just try harder next time!" or, "Maybe it's just not meant for me." Would you believe me if I told you that you have EVERYTHING within yourself to accomplish ANY goal you ever set out to achieve? But until you learn and change what your biggest limiting beliefs are, it is very likely that you wail fail again. And again, and again, and again.

You see, our beliefs are programmed. Just like a computer is. I know that if I hit the long key o the bottom of my keyboard, that it will make a space on the screen while I am writing. That's what the space bar is programmed to do. But if I knew enough about programming, to go in my computer, and reprogram it, so that that long button instead, made a star on the screen, from then on, I would be able to make stars on my screen, and no more spaces! Think about when you think about accomplishing something big - something that may challenge you. 9 times out of 10, that thought is followed, almost immediately, with a "voice" in your head, that will determine right then, if you will be successful or not! You can try to affirm it away. You can try to bulldoze your way through it, but until you REPROGRAM that voice it will continue to play. Remember the subconscious listens to the voice that is the loudest, the most frequent, and has the strongest emotion. For most of us, our limiting beliefs have been playing on a loped tape in our head for many, many, many years! They typically hold deep emotion, which makes the even stronger.

When you develop a deep understanding of how this programming takes place, and more importantly how to reprogram it, the sky truly becomes the limit. Take a minute, and do the exercise on the next page.

Think about a really big goal, dream, or idea that you've had in the past, and didn't accomplish. Write about it below, and then answer the question that follows. Be VERY conscious of the thoughts and voices in your head as you write, and then write them down too. (Be honest)

My goal was: _____
_____
_____
_____

Some reasons that I didn't accomplish it were: _____
_____
_____
_____
_____

As I wrote, these were the thoughts and feelings I had, about the experience: _____
_____
_____
_____
_____
_____
_____
_____

Now, shift gears a little bit. Think about a new goal, dream, or idea that you'd like to accomplish. The sky's the limit! If there were no limitations at all, what would you do?

I would: _____
_____
_____
_____

Some things that I'd have to do in order to accomplish it are: _____
_____
_____
_____
_____

As I wrote, these were the thoughts and feelings I had, about this new goal/dream:_____

_____
_____
_____
_____
_____
_____
_____

Take an inventory for a minute. What did you learn? What were the subconscious reactions you had to each activity? Did any of the thoughts of your previous "failure" bleed into your thoughts about your new dream? How easy was it for you to find all the reasons why you "failed" at the earlier goal? How comfortable were those feelings? Many people live in the looped tape of failure and defeat. Here me when I say this... It's not YOU that is failing! Your "Failures" are simply a result of those darn looped tapes that are programmed to keep you right where you are! Notice the "quotes" around failure. I don't believe there is any such thing as failure... Just lessons to help us improve.

As you started thinking about the "how" of your new dream, did you only think of the excitement, or did any doubts creep in? If your thoughts were all positive, then great! You are a little ahead on the path. Many of us have great feelings when we first have the inspiration, but as we begin thinking about the how, that's when the limiting beliefs start to make themselves known.

If you've done a bit of personal work before, you likely had good thoughts throughout the process. That's great! So I'll give you something to think about. Those of us who are involved in personal development, learned early on to use affirmations and positive thinking. I will only speak for myself, and say that even with all of that training, I still found it challenging to accomplish the really bug stuff! It was incredibly frustrating! I was doing the work! I was visualizing, I was affirming, I had a HUGE vision board! I noticed some things were starting to change, slowly, but a lot of things still seemed to be out of my reach. Then I learned about limiting beliefs, and everything changed!

Let's take a look at what I call, the Flow of Consciousness. When I talked about the levels of consciousness, it flowed UP, from the Conscious to the Subconscious. But now, we are talking about a flow that begins with the Superconscious, and flows into our reality. First, we will look at the IDEAL Flow of Consciousness.

It goes something like this:
1. I get an idea (inspiration) - remember where that comes from?
    "I want to be an Astronaut!"
2. Our idea flows to the Subconscious.
    The Genie says, "Your wish is my command!" and then supports me in setting my life in motion to manifest this dream.
3. Our idea becomes manifest in physical form in our conscious life.
    I become an Astronaut!

The IDEAL Flow of Consciousness

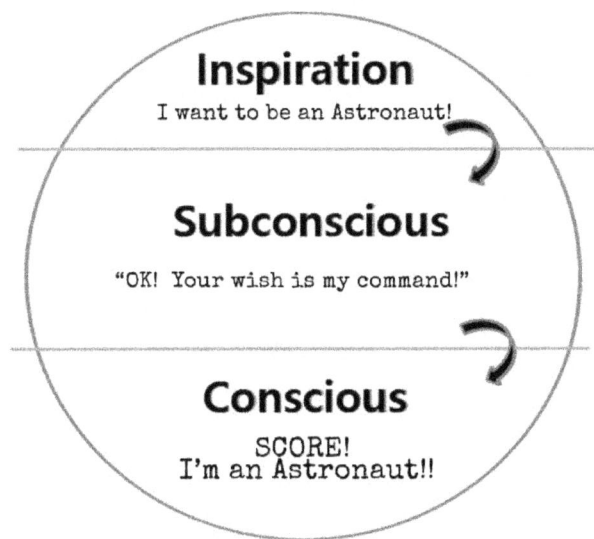

Clearly, if this were how it was in our lives, we would live in the most amazing world we could dream of! (Remember that Utopia I spoke of earlier?) So, let's look at the Flow of Consciousness in reality.

It goes something like this:
1. I get an idea (inspiration) - remember where that comes from?
    "I want to be an Astronaut!"
2. Our idea flows through a filter called our Personal Belief System.
    This is where all of our beliefs live. Both limiting and supporting beliefs are here, so if it's not a real huge idea, or if it's something we have accomplished before, our supportive beliefs kick in to help us accomplish it. But is it's big, scary, or challenging, our limiting beliefs kick in, and the looped tapes begin to play with all the reasons why we can't accomplish it.
3. Our idea flows to the Subconscious.
    The Genie listens to the messages it is hearing that are the loudest, the most frequent, and have the strongest emotion, and says, "Your wish is my command!" and then does what those limiting messages told it to do!
4. Our idea fails, and we have more evidence that we can't.

The REAL Flow of Consciousness

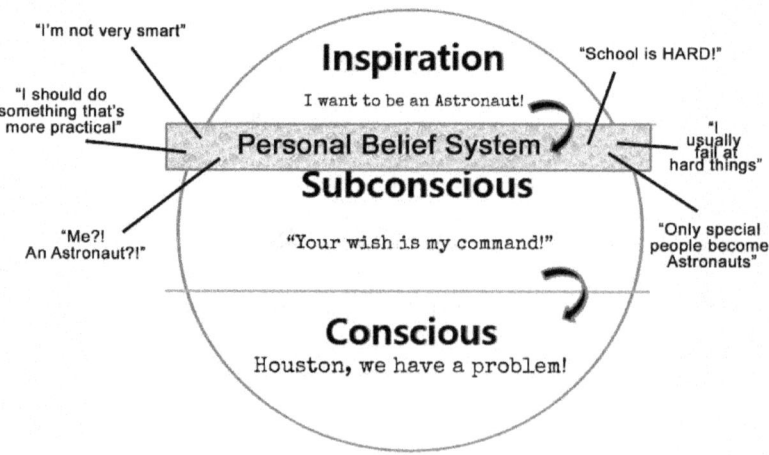

The "hard part" (not really) is to learn how to turn the volume down on those looped tapes, or delete them all together. My goal for you, is that when you are finished with this entire program, you will find that you have and are accomplishing things that used to scare you. You will find it easier to do the big scary stuff, and your very definition of the big scary stuff will be different.

To start the process of breaking through, I invite you to stop reading, until you have competed the exercise below.

First, take a deep breath, close your eyes, and remind yourself how amazing you are! Now, list your top limiting beliefs. What are the things that you truly believe about yourself - not the stuff you tel yourself to get past your limiting beliefs. Be honest. Even the hard stuff that you don't want to admit. List at least 25. More if you can.

_____
_____
_____
_____
_____
_____
_____
_____
_____
_____
_____
_____
_____
_____
_____
_____
_____
_____
_____
_____
_____
_____
_____
_____
_____

Roger Webb

6 - I AM

Now that you got the hard part done, let's start the process of breaking through!

Every spiritual practice on Earth, has a word or phrase that is believed to be powerful, magical, or mystical. This phrase is responsible for many miracles, and is viewed as the ultimate power. Every single one of these phrases, in every single spiritual practice known, translates the same... "I Am." These two words, truly are the most powerful words on Earth. For some they are the highest, most reverent name of God. That's powerful!

Whatever words follow these two words, in your life, in your mind, in your practice - will become your reality. Think for a minute. What follows these two words in your mind, when you think about yourself? What phrases or words follow these two words in your mind, as you go through your day? A wise mentor once asked me, "Roger, would you date someone who talks about you the way that you talk about you?" Holy cow! That was a powerful question! My answer was, "No way! I wouldn't even hang out with them! I wouldn't want them anywhere near me!" I invite you to ask yourself the same question. It's well known that we are our own worst critics. What words and phrases follow "I am..." in your mind? Are they supportive? Are they affirming? Will they lead you to a better place in your life? For some of us, in some areas of our life, it's awesome! Before I did my limiting belief work, I knew without a doubt that I am an amazing dad. I knew that I am an effective coach. But when it came to creating wealth, or reaching big goals, or doing scary stuff, the tapes started to play, "I am scared." "I am a failure." "I am not capable of achieving success." "I am not worthy of success." "I am not deserving of money." no wonder I couldn't accomplish anything big, that led to me attaining wealth! The loudest, the most frequent, and the tapes with the strongest emotion, were looping in my consciousness and my Genie was listening to them!

Are you ready to change them? Are you ready to reprogram those tapes? Are you ready to accomplish amazing, wonderful, powerful, juicy things in your life? This chapter will walk you one of the first, and most powerful steps in breaking through your limiting beliefs. You will create a tool that will support you in creating big magic in your life! I truly believe that this one tool is single-handedly responsible for more success in my life, than anything I have ever done! It's called a Personal Proclamation Statement. If you have completed any of my BBT Bootcamps, then you already have a proclamation statement. It's your choice to edit or change it. I have only made one minor change to mine in over 20 years. It's totally up to you. Follow these simple steps, and you will create a powerful Proclamation Statement that will propel you to amazing places! A few tips before you get started:

> 1. Get support. Getting honest feedback from others who love and care about you, can be invaluable in this process.
>
> 2. Don't rush. It may take a few days of consciously working on this process, until it's right.
>
> 3. Allow your Proclamation Statement be fluid as you read this book and go through the exercises. Your thoughts and feelings may shift as you go through this process. Don't call your Proclamation Statement final until you are ready to start chapter fifteen.
>
> 4. Follow all the steps and advice carefully. Little things matter when you are working with your subconscious.

Step 1: Look at the list of limiting beliefs that you made on pages 23-24. Is it complete? Do you need to add more to it? Get real, get honest, and get deep. What are the things that your limiting beliefs say to you? What are the looped tapes playing? List them all. The more, the better. Be gentle on yourself, but be honest. Know that this part of the process, can be hard and even painful for some people. It's OK. Breathe through it, get support, and know that this ends AMAZING!

Step 2: Underline or highlight the limiting beliefs that you feel have the most power over you.

Step 3: Complete this statement, at least 5-10 times:
"What stops me in life is..." The things that stop you aren't necessarily limiting beliefs. Some examples of the things that stop me in life: My kids, My job, Money, My partner, Not enough time, etc... Get the idea?

What stops me in life is: _____

What stops me in life is: _____

What stops me in life is: _____

What stops me in life is: _____

What stops me in life is: _____

What stops me in life is: _____

What stops me in life is: _____

What stops me in life is: _____

What stops me in life is: _____

What stops me in life is: _____

What stops me in life is: _____

What stops me in life is: _____

What stops me in life is: _____

Step 4: Underline, highlight, or mark the things in Step 3 that have the most power in your life. What's holding you back the most? (2-3 things)

Step 5: Make a list of all the things that you underlined in Steps 2 & 4 in Column A on the next page.

Step 6: In Column B, list a word or words that are the opposite of the word in Column A. For example, if you have the word "unworthy" in Column A ,then you can put "worthy" in Column B. If you have the word "afraid" in Column A ,then you can put "fearless" in Column B. Choose words for Column B that are juicy, powerful words that evoke emotion when you say or hear them. Use a thesaurus if you need to.

Column A

Column B

Step 7: Mark, Highlight, or circle the words in Column B that have the most emotional impact on you.

Step 8: Create your Proclamation Statement, using the words that you put in Column B. Focus on the words that you circled in Column B. Use the following format:

"I am a/an _____, _____, _____ man/woman/leader;
_____(Action statement)_____ now!"

I will tell you my Proclamation Statement as an example:
"I am a dynamic, fearless, worthy man; empowering mankind to live lives of passion, authenticity, and love now!"

Use words from Column B for the first 3 descriptive words. Select words that are a challenge. Select words that you don't believe, but want to. Select words might make you feel a little nauseous. You might need to play around with several combinations before you find the right mix.

In selecting man, woman, or leader, choose the one that you are striving to become more of... The one you identify with the least. Or if there is another word that fits better for you, than these three, go for it!

For your action statement, you can use something that speaks to some of the things that stop you in life (Step 3), or an action that will overcome a big limiting belief, or an action that shows you actively creating or living a life as you desire it to be. The sky is the limit.

Some tips to make your Proclamation Statement a little more powerful:

1. Keep it ACTIVE person - what I mean by that is NOT saying something like "I am a fearless, worthy, passionate man, who is creating a life of magic and abundance now!" Leave out words like "who is" "that is" etc. Instead, "I am a fearless, worthy, passionate man; creating a life of magic and abundance now!" It makes it more about YOU and what YOU are dong now. "Who is" separates you from the statement.

2. Make your statement about your LIFE, not about your BUSINESS. This

is not a business development course. It's a PERSONAL development program. Work on your LIFE and your business will change.

3. Stick to the format suggested. There are several reasons. If you get too long, it complicates it. See where one word could cover the energy of multiple words you are stuck on.

4. Use "juicy" words... words that stir passion and emotion!

5. Make sure it's all about YOU, not others. Change yourself and you will change those round you.

6. Ask people who know you to help. This statement is to bring out the VERY best that you aspire to be!

7. When it makes you feel uneasy, scared, nauseous, etc. You have hit it. This should NOT be a comfortable thing for you to say. If it is, keep reworking it. I have had clients who couldn't even speak it out loud initially. And with that said, you don't have to be at that extreme either. This statement is something you aspire to be. Not something that you already are.

Now that you have your statement, or at least a really good working draft of it (remember, you need to be complete with it before you start on chapter fifteen), here are some tips for success in using your Proclamation:

- Say it at least 10 times a day for 90 days
- Say it to yourself in the mirror. Look into your own eyes. You are the one who needs to believe it the most. For some people, it's very hard to look themselves in the eyes. If it is difficult for you, I absolutely recommend that you do this daily.
- If you really want to make it more powerful, say it in the mirror naked! (what?! Yes! Really, I did just say that. Most people are very uncomfortable looking at themselves in the mirror at all. Being naked takes it to a very personal and intimate place with yourself!)
- Say it OUT LOUD, not to yourself
- Memorize it as soon as possible.
- Use triggers. A trigger is something to remind you to say it. For example, this week, your trigger is your car keys. Every time you touch your car keys, you have to say it. Get a new trigger every week.

- Get support. Tell those in your life who love and care about you, what you are doing. Ask them to support you. Ask them to ask you what your proclamation is often.
- Write it on your bathroom mirror with a dry erase marker! Every time you see it, say it!
- Make several signs with your Proclamation Statement on them. Hang them up around the house. Say it whenever you see it.
- Put a Post-It note on the rear view mirror of your car with your Proclamation Statement on it! When you see it, say it!

Remember, the messages that your Genie hears, are the loudest, the most frequent, and the ones with the strongest emotion. Make it so that your Proclamation Statement is each one of those things, and you WILL see changes begin to occur in your life!

One important note, when doing work with the subconscious. As long as you are feeding it the right messages, change WILL occur. It may not always be noticeable, but it was very common for my clients to call me a few months or years later and say.. "Holy Cow! It's like I woke up and realized my life is in a completely different place than it was when we started!" Your biggest job is to begin listening. Listen to the small ideas that you start to get. Especially the ones that aren't something that the old you would do. Those are course corrections from y our subconscious to take you to a place that supports the new messages it is getting. The more you listen, and do, the more your subconscious sees that you are on board, and will guide you to more changes. The next thing you know, you will wake up and be in a new, powerful, more successful place in your life!

I have crossed paths with many people over the years, who have pushed through and achieved results. Although they have some success in some areas of their lives, they still struggle in other areas. My life's work is to support you to not just "push through" your limiting beliefs, but to truly breakthrough and overcome them. In over 20+ years of coaching, there are common themes that I have found in the area of limiting beliefs. The next 6 chapters will cover these concepts that I believe are very important to truly breakthrough your limiting beliefs. Once you have your Proclamation Statement, and are armed with the information and tools in the coming chapters, you will have everything you need, to realize your dreams!

I want to take just a moment while we are on this topic to talk about lies. Much of what we believe about ourselves, our lives, our abilities, and our talents are LIES! Remember those perceptions? Rarely are they true. More often than not, we begin to form our beliefs based on imperfect interactions with imperfect people, and the stories that develop in our minds are most likely based on lies!

Before we go on, I want to remind you of the TRUTH. The truth about you. The truth about who you are, and what you are capable of. The Divine, Universal truth about you, is that you are perfect. You have access to infinite power, understanding and ability to create. Regardless of what you do or don't believe in spiritually, I think most can agree that we come into this world perfect. We get our start in an amazing body capable of amazing things, with a mind that is capable of computing, planning, loving, calculating, and discovering more wonder than we can even fathom. It is only when we begin experiencing life with others that we lose the clarity of our Divinity and perfection!

Dr. Wayne Dyer stated it so clearly, "You are a Divine creation--a being of light who showed up here as a human being at the exact moment you were supposed to. You are the beloved, a miracle, a part of the eternal perfection." Spiritual leaders and philosophers for centuries have said similar things. Buddha, Jesus, Osho, Gandhi, The Dalai Lama, Mohammed... they all taught of of our Divine birthright. Every spiritual practice known to man, reminds us of our Divinity, our power, our claim to all that is amazing in the Universe! So, why are we living our lives listening to the lies that are plating in our heads?! You are powerful! You are special! You are worthy! You are capable of creating any magic in your life that you desire! But first, you have to stop listening to the lies! My hope is that through the next few chapters, you will be reminded of how amazing you really are, and the lies will have less and less power over you!

7 - THE PRICES WE PAY

In order to truly prepare yourself mentally, emotionally, and spiritually to breakthrough, you first need to get to a place where you are ready to take on these beliefs. It takes some mental fortitude. If you haven't figured it out by now, this journey is not lined with roses and daisies! Personal work can be hard. It can be scary. It can get bloody. You have to want it. You have to have something driving you. You need something to push you through when it's tough. When you are in a place of "enough is enough" you are much more likely to make it through. Only then, AFTER you have cried, AFTER you have healed, AFTER you brush of the dust, will you find a life that is indeed lined with roses, daisies, and a lot of other amazing stuff!

I can usually know when a client walks into my office for the first time, if they will make it through to the other side, or if they will give up when it gets hard. The distinguishing factor is their attitude. When they are sick and tired of living a life they don't want to be living, and are exhausted, but ready to fight... When they are done... When they are fed up, and see no other option than breaking through, no matter how hard it gets, or whatever it takes... Then I know they will succeed.

Many of us aren't quite there, so I have an exercise that will hopefully get you to the place that you are ready to do this, no matter what. Prior to picking up this book, you might have been aware that *something* is stopping you. You may have been aware that *something* has to change. But most people aren't truly aware of all that their limiting beliefs have cost them in their life. These beliefs cost us relationships, love, marriages, failed businesses, living a life of poverty, low self-esteem, failed jobs, staying in jobs that we hate... The list can go on and on.

Take some quiet time to complete the following exercise. Please don't do it in just a few minutes you have in the waiting room at the doctors office, or at the gym. Take some quiet alone time, in an environment where you are safe to go to some deep emotional places. It may take you several sessions to feel complete in this activity. Take as long as you need. In fact, I would recommend that you take at least 30 minutes a day, for 5-7 days to really allow yourself the time to do this right.

Begin by identifying your top 10 limiting beliefs from the list you wrote on pages 23-24. If you want to take on more than 10, go for it! Then one belief at a time, complete the following activity:

#1 - Limiting Belief: _____

#1 - These are the things that this limiting belief has cost me in my life:
_____
_____
_____
_____
_____
_____

#2 - Limiting Belief: _____

#2 - These are the things that this limiting belief has cost me in my life:
_____
_____
_____
_____
_____
_____

#3 - Limiting Belief: _____

#3 - These are the things that this limiting belief has cost me in my life:
_____
_____
_____
_____
_____
_____

#4 - Limiting Belief: _____
_____

#4 - These are the things that this limiting belief has cost me in my life:
_____
_____
_____
_____
_____
_____

#5 - Limiting Belief: _____
_____

#5 - These are the things that this limiting belief has cost me in my life:
_____
_____
_____
_____
_____
_____

#6 - Limiting Belief: _____
_____

#6 - These are the things that this limiting belief has cost me in my life:
_____
_____
_____
_____
_____
_____

#7 - Limiting Belief: _____
_____

#7 - These are the things that this limiting belief has cost me in my life:
_____
_____
_____
_____
_____
_____

#8 - Limiting Belief: _____
_____

#8 - These are the things that this limiting belief has cost me in my life:
_____
_____
_____
_____
_____
_____

#9 - Limiting Belief: _____
_____

#9 - These are the things that this limiting belief has cost me in my life:
_____
_____
_____
_____
_____
_____

#10 - Limiting Belief: _____
_____

#10 - These are the things that this limiting belief has cost me in my life:
_____
_____
_____
_____
_____
_____

Congratulations! That part can be very difficult for some people! Now, read through all 10 of them, and take the time to really process and understand how much these limited beliefs have collectively cost you! Take 20-30 minutes to journal your thoughts and feelings. Make sure that when you are wrapping up, that you write about your feelings of finally being done with the power and influence that these beliefs have had in your life!

_____
_____
_____
_____
_____
_____
_____
_____
_____
_____
_____
_____
_____
_____
_____
_____
_____
_____
_____
_____
_____
_____
_____
_____

In chapter twelve you will be given the opportunity to really turn this around and paint the picture of a future without these limiting beliefs! Bit first, before I hand over the paintbrush, I want to arm you with a few more tools to prepare you for this amazing and wonderful journey.

Stop for a minute. Close your eyes. Take a deep breath or two. Acknowledge yourself for the work you have done thus far. Gregg Braden teaches that very act of you striving to be something more in your life, is the biological signal to your body to begin creating change in your neuro pathways. Just by opening this book, and participating in the activities prior to this, you have signaled to your brain, your body, your cells, and all that you are, that change is happening! Taking this step, actually physically began to change you you are, and it has prepared your whole being to be ready to change! That's SO exciting!

8 - GETTING TO THE ROOT

Remember the experience that Mitch had? What allowed him to resolve and breakthrough the limiting belief that he had, was being able to discover the root of where that belief came from. We continued to dig deeper and deeper, until we discovered the first perception that was at the root of that belief.

This part of the process can be challenging for some. Some of our beliefs are rooted in trauma, or experiences that happened at a very young age. I invite you to do your best. I advise you that you should go slow and easy in this part of the process. I would recommend to you that if you feel like you need some help discovering the roots, that you reach out for help. There is no shame in it. For some reason there is a stigma in the world today about someone seeking professional help to navigate through life's emotional roller coaster. I am deeply rooted in the belief that everyone needs a guide! We ALL have things in our lives to work through.

If you are already seeing someone, and they are effective - keep seeing them, and ask them to support you in this part of the journey. If you are not, I would recommend that you seek out someone who is trained in working with the subconscious. There are many modalities of healing the subconscious... NLP, Hypnotherapy, Timeline Therapy, EMDR, Past Life Regression... Find the one that works for you, and use it! There is a small list of practitioners that I know, trust, and recommend, found in the resource section of bbtguru.com. I get no kickback from any of them. And I recommend any and all of them.

With all of that said, now that I have scared you away from going further, I invite you to re-engage with this process, take a deep breath, and know that many (in fact, most) of my clients and Bootcamp participants have been able to navigate through this part, with success, on their own! I just want to make sure that you know, if something does come up for you that makes this a challenge, there is help available.

Before you begin this next exercise, I would first suggest as before, that you devote some good, quality, quiet time to this activity. It's ok to take a week or so to go through all of this. Don't be in a hurry. Do it right. You have a lifetime to make amazing things happen. The deeper you go here, the more power you will have to overcome your limiting beliefs! Before you start each session of journaling & discovery, I would suggest that you take a few quiet minutes, take some deep breaths, and visualize a beautiful white light surrounding you, protecting you, and guiding you to the truth that lies under each of these limiting beliefs. Sit for a few minutes, wrapped in the warmth of this healing light. Feel it in your cells. When you feel ready, pick up the pen, and go to work!

Now for the exercise. Using the same ten limiting beliefs that you used on page 34, complete the exercise, starting on the next page:

For each limiting belief, name it, and then take some time to think and reflect about it. Where did it come from? In what parts of your life is it triggered the most? Do certain people, environments, or experiences trigger it? When you close your eyes, take a deep breath and think about that belief, who are the people that come to mind? Where are the places you remember? Start with these thoughts and see where you go with it. The further back you can trace a thought, feeling, belief, or experience, you will begin to discover the root perceptions that you had which created these beliefs. Maybe it was something someone said or did. Maybe it was the way you felt after something happened. This chapter requires a lot of contemplation, meditation, prayer, etc. Allow yourself to open up to the learning that your subconscious has in store for you. If it becomes hard, keep going. Allow the tears to fall. Allow yourself to feel, experience, and process everything.

Stop at the realization of the roots of your beliefs. The next chapter will support you in re-framing them, and closing them up.

#1 - Limiting Belief: _____
_____

#1 - Where did this belief come from?

#2 - Limiting Belief: _____

#2 - Where did this belief come from?

#3 - Limiting Belief: _____
_____

#3 - Where did this belief come from?

#4 - Limiting Belief: _____

#4 - Where did this belief come from?

#5 - Limiting Belief: _____
_____

#5 - Where did this belief come from?
_____

#6 - Limiting Belief: _____

#6 - Where did this belief come from?

#7 - Limiting Belief: _____

#7 - Where did this belief come from?

#8 - Limiting Belief: _____

#8 - Where did this belief come from?

#9 - Limiting Belief: _____

_____

#9 - Where did this belief come from?

#10 - Limiting Belief: _____

#10 - Where did this belief come from?

Whew!! Take a deep breath! You did it! That part can be very difficult for some people! Now, read through all 10 of them, and take the time to really process and understand the reality, that these are not YOUR truths! In the next chapter, you are going to work on re-framing each one of them, to bring it into a greater, safer, more healthy place of understanding, that will empower you to heal and move forward into a new and exciting place! Take 20-30 minutes to journal your thoughts and feelings after completing this exercise.

_____
_____
_____
_____
_____
_____
_____
_____
_____
_____
_____
_____
_____
_____
_____
_____
_____
_____
_____
_____
_____
_____
_____
_____
_____
_____
_____
_____
_____
_____

Put Down the Book and DO Something!

9 - RE-FRAMING PERCEPTIONS

Uncovering the roots of your limiting beliefs can be a difficult and painful process for many. I have a tremendous amount of personal respect for those who are willing to do this level of work! Now you have the amazing opportunity to reframe those perceptions. When I was doing my work, this is the step that brought the most clarity and understanding for me. This is the step that helped me move out of sorrow, anger, frustration, and resentment. This is where I found hope. This is where I learned to dream again!

When Mitch uncovered the root of his challenges with his father, it brought with it an opportunity for him to heal, move on, and dis-empower the beliefs (the lies) that he had held onto for so many years!

The re-framing came, as he was able to look at that root perception, with the experience, and context that 35 years of life gave him. He was able to look at the situation with compassion for his father. He was able to see that there was much more to the situation than he was aware of as a 4 year old boy.

When a belief lives in our subconscious it is often filed away in the wrong place. Imagine a library, with rows and rows of shelves. The emotions associated with these beliefs and experiences, caused our subconscious to file them onto the wrong shelves. The location they are filed, when triggered, bring up undesirable feelings and actions that are wrongly associated with them. I hope that makes sense! When we expose our subconscious to the truth about these perceptions, it too, has the capacity of seeing the truth, and the very action of seeing it differently... Of seeing it with new eyes and new understanding allows that memory or perception to get refiled to the correct place.

So in Mitch's experience, all his life, seeing his dad, talking to his dad, or even hearing his dad's name, triggered feelings of sadness, anger, and resentment... Because that is where it was filed. As soon as he had his new understanding around the situation, the truth was exposed, and the subconscious had no choice but to file that memory instead in the shelf that holds memories of his childhood that were insignificant. Now that it's reshelved, when Mitch sees his father, or hears his name, he only feels love. It's really that easy.

Now you have the opportunity to work on re-framing each of the perceptions that you uncovered in the previous chapter. This is one of my favorite parts of this work! I received some amazing gifts and insights as I went through this process for the first time!

We are going to now take your same top 10 limiting beliefs, and work on each one. Refer back to the things you discovered about each one, in the previous chapter.

As always, prior to starting this exercise, make sure that you are in a quiet environment that will allow you to be fully present. Close your eyes, take a few long, slow, deep breaths, and open your ind to the possibilities that await you as you begin to reframe these perceptions.

Begin the activity on the next page, and answer each of the suggested questions for each limiting belief.

#1 - Limiting Belief: _____

_____

Looking at the root that you discovered on page 42, answer the following questions:

With my current understanding, what do I know to be true about that perception that I may not have known then? _____

_____
_____
_____
_____
_____

What are the positive gifts, qualities, or traits that I have today, as a result of that experience? _____

_____
_____
_____
_____
_____
_____

What advice would I give to myself at that age, in regards to this experience? _____

_____
_____
_____
_____
_____
_____

What is a Universal truth that I know deep inside myself, that proves this belief to be false? _____

_____
_____
_____
_____

#2 - Limiting Belief: _____
_____

Looking at the root that you discovered on page 43, answer the following questions:

With my current understanding, what do I know to be true about that perception that I may not have known then? _____
_____
_____
_____
_____
_____
_____

What are the positive gifts, qualities, or traits that I have today, as a result of that experience? _____
_____
_____
_____
_____
_____
_____
_____

What advice would I give to myself at that age, in regards to this experience?   _____
_____
_____
_____
_____
_____
_____
_____

What is a Universal truth that I know deep inside myself, that proves this belief to be false? _____
_____
_____
_____
_____
_____

#3 - Limiting Belief: _____

_____

Looking at the root that you discovered on page 44, answer the following questions:

With my current understanding, what do I know to be true about that perception that I may not have known then? _____

_____
_____
_____
_____
_____
_____

What are the positive gifts, qualities, or traits that I have today, as a result of that experience? _____

_____
_____
_____
_____
_____
_____
_____

What advice would I give to myself at that age, in regards to this experience? _____

_____
_____
_____
_____
_____
_____

What is a Universal truth that I know deep inside myself, that proves this belief to be false? _____

_____
_____
_____
_____

#4 - Limiting Belief: _____

_____

Looking at the root that you discovered on page 45, answer the following questions:

With my current understanding, what do I know to be true about that perception that I may not have known then? _____

_____
_____
_____
_____
_____
_____

What are the positive gifts, qualities, or traits that I have today, as a result of that experience? _____

_____
_____
_____
_____
_____
_____

What advice would I give to myself at that age, in regards to this experience? _____

_____
_____
_____
_____
_____
_____

What is a Universal truth that I know deep inside myself, that proves this belief to be false? _____

_____
_____
_____
_____

#5 - Limiting Belief: _____

_____

Looking at the root that you discovered on page 46, answer the following questions:

With my current understanding, what do I know to be true about that perception that I may not have known then? _____

_____
_____
_____
_____
_____
_____

What are the positive gifts, qualities, or traits that I have today, as a result of that experience? _____

_____
_____
_____
_____
_____
_____

What advice would I give to myself at that age, in regards to this experience?   _____

_____
_____
_____
_____
_____
_____

What is a Universal truth that I know deep inside myself, that proves this belief to be false? _____

_____
_____
_____
_____
_____

#6 - Limiting Belief: _____
_____

Looking at the root that you discovered on page 47, answer the following questions:

With my current understanding, what do I know to be true about that perception that I may not have known then? _____
_____
_____
_____
_____
_____
_____

What are the positive gifts, qualities, or traits that I have today, as a result of that experience? _____
_____
_____
_____
_____
_____
_____

What advice would I give to myself at that age, in regards to this experience?   _____
_____
_____
_____
_____
_____
_____

What is a Universal truth that I know deep inside myself, that proves this belief to be false? _____
_____
_____
_____
_____
_____

#7 - Limiting Belief: _____
_____

Looking at the root that you discovered on page 48, answer the following questions:

With my current understanding, what do I know to be true about that perception that I may not have known then? _____
_____
_____
_____
_____
_____
_____

What are the positive gifts, qualities, or traits that I have today, as a result of that experience? _____
_____
_____
_____
_____
_____
_____
_____

What advice would I give to myself at that age, in regards to this experience? _____
_____
_____
_____
_____
_____
_____

What is a Universal truth that I know deep inside myself, that proves this belief to be false? _____
_____
_____
_____
_____
_____

#8 - Limiting Belief: _____
_____

Looking at the root that you discovered on page 49, answer the following questions:

With my current understanding, what do I know to be true about that perception that I may not have known then? _____
_____
_____
_____
_____
_____

What are the positive gifts, qualities, or traits that I have today, as a result of that experience? _____
_____
_____
_____
_____
_____
_____

What advice would I give to myself at that age, in regards to this experience?   _____
_____
_____
_____
_____
_____
_____

What is a Universal truth that I know deep inside myself, that proves this belief to be false? _____
_____
_____
_____
_____

#9 - Limiting Belief: _____

_____

Looking at the root that you discovered on page 50, answer the following questions:

With my current understanding, what do I know to be true about that perception that I may not have known then? _____

_____
_____
_____
_____
_____
_____

What are the positive gifts, qualities, or traits that I have today, as a result of that experience? _____

_____
_____
_____
_____
_____
_____
_____

What advice would I give to myself at that age, in regards to this experience?   _____

_____
_____
_____
_____
_____
_____

What is a Universal truth that I know deep inside myself, that proves this belief to be false? _____

_____
_____
_____
_____
_____

#10 - Limiting Belief: _____
_____

Looking at the root that you discovered on page 51, answer the following questions:

With my current understanding, what do I know to be true about that perception that I may not have known then? _____
_____
_____
_____
_____
_____

What are the positive gifts, qualities, or traits that I have today, as a result of that experience? _____
_____
_____
_____
_____
_____
_____

What advice would I give to myself at that age, in regards to this experience? _____
_____
_____
_____
_____
_____
_____

What is a Universal truth that I know deep inside myself, that proves this belief to be false? _____
_____
_____
_____
_____
_____

Hopefully, you were able to find some new and powerful truths about yourself during that process. I invite you to take about 15-20 minutes to answer the following question. What do I now know to be true about me, my life, my experiences, and what I am capable of creating from this moment forward in my life? _____

_____
_____
_____
_____
_____
_____
_____
_____
_____
_____
_____
_____
_____
_____
_____
_____
_____
_____
_____
_____
_____
_____
_____
_____
_____
_____
_____
_____
_____
_____
_____
_____
_____
_____

10 - BUILDING MASSIVE EVIDENCE

This is, in my opinion the most fun part of this whole process! There are few things more gratifying to me than proving a limiting belief wrong! So much of the work you have done up to this point has been chipping away at these limiting beliefs. You may have even found that some of them are already gone, because of the work you have already done! One of the best ways to completely blow up a limiting belief, is to create massive evidence that it is WRONG! I use the word "massive" on purpose. It needs to be big! It needs to be powerful! It needs to invoke deep emotion! It needs to be extraordinary! Smaller actions will work, but it may take several of these small actions, and they may not be as long lasting.

One of my biggest, baddest, most ruthless beliefs for most of my life, was that I was afraid. Fear ran me. Fear of success. Fear of what others will think. Fear of dying. Fear. Plain and simple. I didn't jump off of high dives because I as afraid. I didn't do flips on the trampoline because I was afraid. I didn't take ANY risks in my life, because I was afraid. This fear cost me millions. It cost me failed businesses, it cost me always being someone else's #2 because I was afraid to be my own #1. It kept me living a very mediocre life, because I was afraid of getting any more than that.

Then, at midnight, on December 23, 2013, I jumped 855 feet off of the top of the Las Vegas Stratosphere! It was hands down, the most terrifying moment of my life. At the top. Before I jumped, I told the woman working, that I would not open my eyes, and she'd have to guide me through the steps. I couldn't look. But I had promised myself, that when she said "jump" that I would jump! UGH. It was dark, and a little breezy. I made the mistake of opening my eyes, and got a glimpse of what was around me. I was standing on a platform that seemed to be about 4 feet wide, much like a diving platform, and I was 855 feet in the air! I immediately closed my eyes, in an effort to keep my stomach contents in check. I remember reaching for the bars to hold on to, having a little challenge finding them with my eyes closed. She buckled me in to the cable, and told me to walk over and put my toes over the edge of the platform. UGH. I had to open my eyes, and even worse, I had to look down, to see where to put my toes. My heart was in my throat. All I remember is hearing her say, "OK - Here we go... 3... 2... 1" and I jumped! SHEER TERROR for about 2 seconds, and then I discovered I was flying. I DID IT! I FREAKING DID IT! My screams of terror turned into screams of joy! PURE JOY! I looked fear in the eyes, and said, "I WIN!"   30 seconds later, my feet touched down, and I couldn't contain my excitement! It was truly the most powerful single moment of my life. Later that night, when I told someone what I had done, she looked at me and said, "Dang! You're a badass!" My only thought was, "Yes! You're right! I am!"

My life changed that day. Any time fear has shown up, it's immediately replaced with the memory of me flying through the Las Vegas sky, and my only thought, is, "I'm a badass! Not today fear! Not today!" Since then, I have built 2 very successful businesses, and am working on a third. I have watched my kids accomplish amazing things, because they too now have evidence that fear is not real, and that we truly can do anything we want to do! I created MASSIVE evidence that I am not afraid!

I am a serial entrepreneur. I always have been. At 12 years old, I was the youngest member ever, of the American Rabbit Breeders Association. I had a thriving middle school business, and I got a taste of what it meant to work for myself, and be my own boss. It set me off on a lifetime of entrepreneurial ventures. Some moderately successful, but most of them were failures.   There are a million opportunities out there, and I tried about half of them! Although I did ok, I never quite made it. I was never able to achieve the success that I desired. When I started my personal work, I learned that I had a deeply rooted belief that I was incapable of achieving success. I was really good at getting "almost there," but never quite "there." I wanted to be the guy who finally got the big check. I realized that it was less about the money, and more about proving to myself that I WAS CAPABLE! I needed to have proof that I was indeed worthy of that kind of a life. (Another deep belief that I had.) So I did my work. I did all the things that I'm asking you to do. I began chipping away at these limiting beliefs. I worked hard! I went to workshops and retreats. I learned to visualize and employ as many subconscious tools as possible.

I had tried the MLM thing MANY times in the past, and with each failure. I become more convinced that they were all a miserable way to lose money! A few years ago, a good friend of mine shared her "opportunity" with me. Initially I was very closed minded. I wasn't about to let failure win again. But the circumstances of my life at the time, were such that I really needed SOMETHING to make a better living for myself and my kids. I'm a single dad, raising 5 kids on my own. Life was tough. I had done my work around these beliefs, and I saw a possible opportunity to show my kids that you really can create your own success. So I decided to give MLMs one more chance, believing that with my NEW tools, and my NEW understandings and insights, that I could indeed have success. As soon as I said yes, the voices started playing! All my previous failures played out in my mind. I was ready. I had the tools, and I knew that I could win if I used them! So I went to work. I worked hard. I had some really strong motivation pushing me along, but the strongest was my determination to prove to myself that I was indeed worthy and capable of being "That guy" who made it!

Interesting fact is, that I said yes, just a few months after jumping off the Stratosphere! (See what happens when we take all these beliefs on at once! I was no longer afraid to go for it!) My goal was to become a Diamond, one of the highest ranks in my company. Diamond is equivalent to all the ranks I had attempted in other businesses, and failed trying. It was time to build massive evidence, so that these beliefs no longer had control over me! 20 months after I started, I achieved the rank of Diamond! It was one of the of my greatest achievements! About 8 months later, at the international convention, I was celebrated at our annual Gala, where I walked across the stage hearing my name called, hearing MY SONG played, and hearing my friends, loved ones, and many of my mentors, cheering me on! It was a very powerful moment! It was a moment that is burned int my brain. Now, any time I get a glimpse of that "I'm not worthy," or "I'm not capable" program, I am able to laugh in it's face, remember the moment I was on that stage and shout back "YES I AM!!!" And with that, they shut up, and I can go on creating more amazing magic in my life! I created MASSIVE evidence that they are wrong! Evidence that moves me deeply. Evidence that I can PROVE without a doubt, that these beliefs have NO power over me!

So this activity is fun! Follow the directions starting on the next page. Again we are working with the same top ten limiting beliefs. (I hope some of them are already getting weaker!)

#1 - Limiting Belief: _____
_____

#1 - List 5 activities that you can do to prove this belief wrong. The bigger the better!
1. _____
2. _____
3. _____
4. _____
5. _____

#2 - Limiting Belief: _____
_____

#2 - List 5 activities that you can do to prove this belief wrong. The bigger the better!
1. _____
2. _____
3. _____
4. _____
5. _____

#3 - Limiting Belief: _____
_____

#3 - List 5 activities that you can do to prove this belief wrong. The bigger the better!
1. _____
2. _____
3. _____
4. _____
5. _____

#4 - Limiting Belief: _____
_____

#4 - List 5 activities that you can do to prove this belief wrong. The bigger the better!
1. _____
2. _____
3. _____
4. _____
5. _____

#5 - Limiting Belief: _____
_____

#5 - List 5 activities that you can do to prove this belief wrong. The bigger the better!
1. _____
2. _____
3. _____
4. _____
5. _____

#6 - Limiting Belief: _____
_____

#6 - List 5 activities that you can do to prove this belief wrong. The bigger the better!
1. _____
2. _____
3. _____
4. _____
5. _____

#7 - Limiting Belief: _____
_____

#7 - List 5 activities that you can do to prove this belief wrong. The bigger the better!
1. _____
2. _____
3. _____
4. _____
5. _____

#8 - Limiting Belief: _____
_____

#8 - List 5 activities that you can do to prove this belief wrong. The bigger the better!
1. _____
2. _____
3. _____
4. _____
5. _____

#9 - Limiting Belief: _____
_____

#9 - List 5 activities that you can do to prove this belief wrong. The bigger the better!
1. _____
2. _____
3. _____
4. _____
5. _____

#10 - Limiting Belief: _____

_____

#10 - List 5 activities that you can do to prove this belief wrong. The bigger the better!
1. _____
2. _____
3. _____
4. _____
5. _____

You now have FIFTY amazing things that you can do to begin to blow these beliefs out of the water. I hope you picked some big ones! The bigger and scarier they are, the more effective they will be! You have everything inside of you to do this! Your challenge now, is to DO THEM! My advice would be to pick the biggest and scariest first! Get them out of the way!

Remember, taking a step towards bettering your life sends a biological signal to your body to begin rebuilding the neurons that control these behaviors! Take a step! Put something on the calendar. Make an appointment to do something on this list. Make that phone call... write that letter... Take the first step TODAY!

11 - LOVING YOURSELF UNCONDITIONALLY

Let's break this topic down into two parts, and then put them together.

1. Loving yourself... What does that mean? Not the stuff you read on that great Meme on Social Media. Not the things that your personal growth gurus have all said. Truly loving yourself goes deep. Deeper than most of us are comfortable going with ourselves. Think of someone or something in your life that you truly love (or loved) with all of your heart and soul. Think about the feelings you have for them. Feel the emotions as you recall the memories, feelings, experiences that you shared together. You might even go so far as to write them down. Now, I invite you to do n inventory on your feelings about yourself. Do those same feelings, emotions, and thoughts apply to yourself, in relationship to yourself? If not, why not? There is no one on this Earth who deserves your love, more than you do! I invite you to make an inventory, a list, of the qualities and traits that you love about yourself. My wish for you, is that it is a very long list, and comes to you easily. If not, I suggest there might be some work that needs done in this area. We will explore in a but, some things you can do to strengthen the love and feelings that you have for yourself.

2. Unconditional... This is a loaded word. It's my opinion (and maybe even a little judgment), that this word is thrown around in ting or thought as to what it really means. In the literal context, it means to have NO conditions. None. Zero. Zilch. When we, as mortal human beings talk about loving unconditionally, I don't think we have the first clue, what that really means. We say that a mother loves her children unconditionally, and yet when that child does something reprehensible, it affects the love. Was it truly without condition? I do BELIEVE that many of us have true unconditional love towards a very select few in our lives, but I also BELIEVE that it's the exception, not the norm. If it was, there would be little to no divorce or homeless teens. The best example of unconditional love that I can think of, is my dog, Nona. Nona is a very connected, and loving being. When I leave the house, even if it's to run an errand two blocks away, and I'm only gone for 5 minutes, she greets me at the door EVERY time I return, as if I have been gone for months, and she is rejoicing that I am home! This is one

of the reasons, I love dogs so much, and Nona, even more so. She loves me. Even if I scold her for chewing something I love. Even if I forget to feed her. Even if I accidentally lock her in the back yard for hours. She loves me. Period. WITH NO CONDITIONS!

When we are looking at unconditionally loving ourselves, that says a lot! A WHOLE LOT! That means when I screw up, I still love myself. That means that if I'm out of shape and 30 pounds overweight, I still love myself. That means when I make huge, massive mistakes, I still love myself. That means that even when I give myself many reasons to not love me, that I can still greet myself in the mirror like Nona greets me at the door!

Think about it. The only REAL guarantee of ANYONE in your life that you know without a doubt, will ALWAYS be with you, NO MATTER WHAT, is YOU! With that in mind, how do you treat yourself? What kinds of things do you say to yourself? Do you spoil yourself? Do you make yourself laugh? A mentor once said to me, "Would you date someone who speaks about you the way that YOU speak about you?" WOW! That was a powerful question! At the time, I wouldn't even want to hang out with someone who spoke to me the way I spoke about myself, let alone, date them?! Think about those in your life that you love. What are the things that helped to develop that love? It wasn't instant. Love it grown. It requires nurturing, patience, and time. Think about the events, the situations, the experiences that the two of you shared, that allowed that LOVE to grow and flourish. I have a challenge for you. Start a love affair with yourself! Spend time with yourself, laughing, crying, trusting (oh - that's a tough one!) yourself. Take all those events, things, situations, experiences that you had with hose you love, and give yourself those same things with yourself! Court yourself! Yes! I know that sounds crazy, but THAT is how you will begin to develop a deeper love for the ONE person who will ALWAYS be at your side... YOU! Think about those who you love. When they mess up, how do they get back into your good graces? When they wear an outfit that you don't like, do you criticize them? Or do you allow then to be themselves? If you do criticize them or laugh at what they are wearing, is that coming from a place of love, or is it about you and your embarrassment? That's a good way to see if you are truly loving unconditionally. Then turn that inward, and love yourself the same way! Love YOURSELF, the same way (or better) that you love your very closest friend. Give yourself the same leeway to be human as you give your closest friends and loved ones.

It might also be important to look at the WHY behind your treatment of yourself. If you are hard on yourself, why are you? If you are self-critical, why? If you are short and impatient with yourself, ask yourself why you aren't more patient and loving. Our behaviors are shaped by events, experiences, and situations in our lives. Remember the programming I spoke of earlier. Where were you programmed to treat yourself the way that you do? There may be some places to do some powerful healing and reprogramming around this!

I invite you to open up to this idea of unconditional self-love, by doing a simple 3-5 minute exercise. Right now. Put the book down and do this... Go into your bathroom or bedroom, somewhere with a mirror. Close the door, and ensure you have uninterrupted time alone for a few minutes. Then stand in front of the mirror. Look at yourself. REALLY look at yourself. What do you see, what do you notice, where do your thoughts take you? Are you judging yourself? Are you critical of something you see? Are you complimentary? Do you look good? See where your thoughts take you. Then take a minute or two to really connect with that amazing, beautiful, powerful, divine person looking back at you, by looking into their eyes. Really connect, eye to eye. Don't look away. See the light, the pain, the sparkle, the joy... see whatever you see. Give that person permission to see you. No words. Only with your eyes. Then start speaking. Tell that amazing person looking back at you, 5 things that you love and admire about them. Compliment them. Tell them your feelings about them... ONLY THE GOOD STUFF! This is a space for ONLY positive... only love... If you find something negative come up, stop, take a deep breath, and then start again. Spend 2-3 minutes speaking with that person looking back at you. If possible, maintain eye contact the entire time you are talking. If that's hard, work up to it. Imagine that you are across the table from the future love of your life, and you get the chance to paint a picture of your perfect life together. Go there! Allow yourself to connect and love that person in the mirror in a deep, intimate, authentic way... and remember - only love. Only positive. Only happiness and joy. Before you end your time together, make sure you look them in the eye, and close the conversation by simply saying, "I love you." I invite you to repeat this process every single day! Make it a daily ritual of love. I can PROMISE you that if you did this simple 3-5 minute exercise with yourself every day, that you will begin to see amazing shifts in your life, your business, your job, your relationships... in EVERY area of your life! It's time. It's time for you to fall in love with you! If you find this hard, challenging, painful, or scary, then I encourage you do do it anyway! Especially those of you who find this hard! If it is difficult, try doing it the first time without the mirror, or stand in front of the mirror, but close your eyes. Then work up to taking it deeper. If you are a parent, teach your children to do this! It's amazing how different they will grow up, when they learn to love themselves early in life!

There are some other fun and wacky ways that you can begin to develop your self-love. The sky's the limit on things you can do! The easiest way to think about it, is to remember the things that others have done for or to you, to get you to fall in love with them... Did they write you love letters? Did they send you loving texts? Maybe they complimented you, or took you to see amazing things. Perhaps it was the way they laughed at your jokes? Whatever it was, as crazy as this sounds, start doing these things for yourself! Take yourself out on a date! Write yourself love notes! Laugh at/with yourself. Take the time to fall in love with you, and your whole view of the world will change. Those who have mastered this, are those who the world admires, respects, and emulates. One of my favorite celebrities closes every show with the following amazing mantra, "If you can't love yourself, then how the hell are you gonna love someone else?!" I couldn't agree more! Once you truly love yourself, unconditionally, you will begin to see every area of your life improve. You will love deeper, soar higher, and dream bigger, than you ever imagined possible!

12 - LIVING CONSCIOUSLY

Unconscious living, in my opinion is the single greatest threat to our very existence on this Earth. I'm not talking just about individually; I believe this applies across the planet, and affects all of mankind. I believe very strongly, that unconscious living is the #1 cause of homelessness, poverty, hunger, famine, heartache, disconnection, and even war. To me, living consciously, means that we are ACTIVELY aware of our thoughts, our actions, and our words. It means that we consciously know how the effect of our thoughts, our actions, and our words will affect ourselves and others. Conscious living in and of itself, says that I acknowledge my place in this world, and my part in humanity. Conscious living says that I fully understand the effects of my interactions with myself, with others, and with this place we live, called Earth. When we are living consciously, we know the reactions to our actions, and we think about those reactions before we even take the actions that cause them.

When I first began my journey of personal discovery, I participated in a 90 day program in which there was a rule set in place, where I got fined (with money!) for using certain words. If I said "but" or "try" it cost me a dollar, and if I said "can't" I lost a five dollar bill! This was my first big lesson in living consciously. I was broke at the time, and it quickly began costing me a lot of money! I very quickly got to a place where I truly gave thought to every single word that came out of my mouth. I'm so grateful for the lesson this experience taught me. It was so easy to let those words come out of my mouth, without really even thinking about what they meant! Every time I said one of those words, I was defeating myself, often before even starting something!

Then I had the thought, "If my words come out so unconsciously, what about my actions?" Wow. Talk about a wake up call! I began to notice my actions and even my thoughts, and how easily I was allowing them to run on autopilot! I began to see where they were costing me money, relationships, time, opportunities, etc. I started to see where I had allowed circumstances in my life to create new habits, that fired on autopilot, and often without me even being consciously aware of them!

Think about this scenario - You are driving on the freeway. Traffic is stop and go. You may even be running late for something important. Someone cuts you off in traffic, almost causing an accident. How do you react? I would argue that 99% of us, react to this scenario unconsciously. We get angry, we yell, we swear, we shout out insults and names to the other driver, we honk, or we might even get aggressive. All of that us unconscious... habit... programming, if you will. In the book, The Book of Joy: Lasting Happiness in a Changing World, Archbishop Desmond Tutu talks about this very thing. He offers a new perspective to this same scenario. He CHOOSES to believe that the person who cut him off, is rushing to the hospital to be with a loved one, or to welcome the birth of a child, and wishes them safety on their journey! What a powerful lesson in conscious living. He is actively engaged in the thoughts in his mind, and the words that leave his mouth. In the first scenario, which is the most common for many of us, we are left angry, frustrated, & upset. Our reaction affects us. If causes our nervous system to go on edge. It affects our breathing, our heart rate, and releases all kinds of hormones and chemicals into our systems that leave us in a state of dis-ease. The Archbishops reaction, instead leaves him feeling connected, and peaceful. He has chosen to react differently, but that choice first required a consciousness of the need to choose.

My youngest son loves to play board games. One of his favorites, is The Game of Life. He asks me to play it often, and that game has taught me a lot about conscious living. How many of us go through life spinning the wheel, moving to the box, doing what it says, and spinning again?! We go through life living a series of actions vs. choices. We do what we were taught to do. We don't question, we don't challenge ourselves to grow, and we rarely explore or discover new ways of doing and being. We do life just how our parents did life, with few variations. We are zombies. I hate to break it to you, but the apocalypse has already happened. It's happening every day. So many of us go through life doing and saying whatever we have to do and say to make it through and not rock the boat. It's time to WAKE UP! It's time for us to choose our thoughts, our words, and our actions.

When I live consciously, I become aware of how I affect those around me. I begin to see my impact on others, even down to my personal impact on the planet and mankind as a whole! I begin to see that I matter. I begin to know that I am a powerful, amazing, beautiful, divine being capable of anything I want to create in my life! I begin to reprogram my unconscious mind in a way that will overcome challenges, innovate, create, and connect. I now see how my words affect others, and I choose new words. I experience how my actions create reactions and am vividly aware of how that shapes and shifts the world around me. I am now a more connected and important member of the human family, because I am awake and aware.

I have a challenge for you. For one day, or even start with just an hour, do your very best to be consciously aware of your thoughts. Examine them, acknowledge them. Question them. Why are you thinking/feeling that? How is your thought affecting you? How would it affect someone else? Then notice how being conscious of your thoughts, change the things that you say and do. When you speak, stop and give every word conscious thought. Is it communicating what you want it to? Could it be misunderstood? Will your words uplift and make someone or a situation better, or will it hurt, and make the situation worse? Take the time to inspect every action you take. Does this action support your greater cause and mission? Does it lead you or someone else to a greater place? If not, do you want to take it? What will the reactions be if you take this action? Whew! This seems like a LOT right?! Who has the time to do this with every thought, word, or action?! My counter to that would be, "Who has the time NOT to?!" By putting this level of consciousness into practice for just short snippets of time throughout the day, you will be amazed at how easy it becomes. To this day, more than twenty years later, I am not able to say those three words, without catching myself! When consciousness becomes a habit, you will experience life at a higher level of peace and joy than you imagined possible.

A few months ago, I was in Long Beach for a business meeting, one of my adult daughters was with me, and I had one day of meetings that she was not involved with. She met up with some friends and went for a walk on the beach. They noticed an insane amount of trash, and the three of them decided to be good Samaritans and picked up trash. She was quickly made aware of the insane number of green straws littering the beach. She has recently seen a video online of a sea turtle that had a straw lodged in it's nose, and it quickly became clear to her, the damage that was being done by our abundant, and unnecessary use of straws in everything we drink. For the rest of the trip, every time we stopped to eat, when I would reach for a straw, she would remind me of the implications of my overuse of straws. It seems silly, but it's caused me once again to see how I am working on auto pilot. Unconscious of my choices. I lived many years on this planet without the use of a straw to drink, yet here I was, reaching unconsciously for a straw, because that's just the way it's done now. I was using straws without even thinking about what happens to that straw once I'm done with it. Where does it go? What impact does it have on the world? Will it be MY straw that hurts a sea turtle or a bird? To take it deeper... my straw is made of plastic. How is my overuse of plastic affecting our planet? How is my overuse of plastic, programming my kids?! My question for you, is what is your straw? What are the things in your life that you use or do unconsciously, but if you really stopped to think about it, you'd choose a better option that will be beneficial for yourself, for others, and for the Earth?

We all have our "straws." I invite you as you practice conscious living to think big picture. Think long term. Think outside of just the impacts in YOUR life. When we develop the habit of reflection in regards to our thoughts, our words, and our actions, we begin to shift to a higher level of living. Living in a place where we are beginning to realize and manifest the divine truths about ourselves!

Conscious thinking is 90% of the battle in overcoming your limiting beliefs. When you are able to "Cut them off at the pass" in your thoughts, you can stop them, and course correct, before they cause upheaval in your life! When I began to think consciously, I was able to identify and overcome my limiting beliefs much faster, because they were now out in the light. When you can master this ONE thing, you will become the master architect of your life!

13 - WHO ARE YOU & WHAT DO YOU REALLY WANT?

Who are you? On the surface, this is a pretty simple question, but I want to take it a bit deeper. Who are you as a human being? As a man? As a woman? As a child? As a sibling? As a partner? I've found in my work with clients, as well as my own experience, that those who have a very clear self identity, seem to accomplish their goals and dreams more than those who are just existing... going with the flow of life. When I've allowed myself to look very honestly at my life, I have been able to go much deeper in answering this question. I've also found that as aware, awake, and enlightened as you might be, we all have moments in our life, where we slip - where we lose focus on who we are! There are a few things I'd like to dissect with this topic.

The first place I'd like to look, is looking at how you are living your life, in relation to the question "Who are you?" I was recently asked a very powerful question, that rocked my world. "Do you want to go through life, living like a gazelle, or like a lion?" The gazelle is nervous, frantic, lives in fear, always looking for the danger... almost *expecting* the danger. Life for the gazelle is never relaxed and carefree. The lion on the other hand, is confident, strong, clear on it's mission and intention. It hunts, it eats, it basks in the sun. The lion doesn't give a damn what's around the next corner, what's waiting at the water hole, etc. So I ask, which are you, and how is that affecting who you are and how you interact with your day?

One of the most empowering pieces of personal development of my life have been around this next question... "Who are you on this planet? Why are you here? What is your mission?" One of the universal questions of mankind forever, is "Why am I here?" One of my very favorite things in working with my clients, has been the mission work. The work I have done with clients to help them get clear on their own personal missions... helping them to gain clarity on their purpose, their contribution, their reason for being.

Living a mission centered life, allows some awesome things to happen in your life. First, It makes decisions easier. When I used to be faced with a challenging decision in my life, it often brought crazy anxiety and stress. I was always afraid that I was going to make the wrong decision.

Now, it's simple. When I'm faced with a choice to make, I ask one simple question, "Does this support or fit into my mission?" It's either yes or no. This one thing has taken away so much angst in my life!

Next, knowing your purpose, gives you clarity. Clarity in every area of your life. Not only does it make your decisions easier, it creates a new focus that can drive you to accomplish amazing things, much easier than you ever imagined. Things in your life will either fit into your mission and support it, or they won't. This gets rid of so many gray areas!

I have seen many times, that those who are clear on their own personal missions, walk with a much greater level of confidence. We are rock solid in who we are, and what we have to contribute. There is no more room for wishy washy. When I became clear on my mission, I began to accept my contribution to the world in such an amazing and deep way. Others opinions no longer sway me. I know who I am, and that's that. I feel so much more grounded and confident in everything that I do!

Knowing your path, or purpose, creates a resolve that supports you in rising above your limiting beliefs. If I am clear that my mission is to be a powerful and effective leader, then the limiting belief of "I'm not good enough" no longer holds weight with me! If you find that your purpose is to be a healer, there is no more room in life for your "I'm not good enough" belief.

A part of getting clear on what I call your Divine mission and purpose, is identifying what it is, that you really want in your life. This is a process, and hopefully, this chapter will allow you to become much more clear on what it is that you want in your life. What I found for myself, is that once I was clear on what I wanted, it was an easy transition to who I was. My "What I wanted" scared the life out of me, when I first got clear. (I will talk more about my experience later in this chapter.) It was scary, but it resonated with me at a level that I couldn't deny it. Once I had that realization, I couldn't deny what kind of man I would have to be to get what I wanted... That shaped the "who am I" answer into an amazing place.

I invite you to take some quite time to go through this next exercise. Give yourself at least 30 minutes. Don't think ahead. Don't go into this with the end in mind. Be conscious with your answers and be conscious of your thoughts as you go through this process. My hope, is that when you are done, you will have a pretty clear vision around who you are, and what you really want to do with your life. If not, I invite you to repeat the process until you feel like you got it.

Step 1: What do you want? What are your initial/immediate goals and desires in life?

_____
_____
_____
_____
_____
_____
_____
_____
_____
_____
_____
_____
_____

Step 2: Looking at what you wrote above, what form do you see this taking? What does it look like? Paint a picture.

_____
_____
_____
_____
_____
_____
_____
_____
_____
_____
_____
_____
_____

Step 3: Looking at what you just wrote, what feelings or experiences to you want to get from that?

_____

Step 4: Looking at what you wrote above, what do you REALLY want? What is a bigger desire that is underneath that? Why do you want those feelings or experiences?

_____

Step 5: Looking at what you just wrote, what form do you see this taking? What does it look like? Paint a picture.

Step 6: Looking at what you wrote above, what feelings or desires to you want to get from that?

Step 7: Looking at what you just wrote, what do you REALLY want? What is a bigger desire that is underneath that? Why do you want those feelings or experiences?

_____
_____
_____
_____
_____
_____
_____
_____
_____
_____
_____
_____

Step 8: Looking at what you wrote above, what form do you see this taking? What does it look like? Paint a picture.

_____
_____
_____
_____
_____
_____
_____
_____
_____
_____
_____
_____
_____
_____

Step 9: Looking at what you wrote above, what feelings or desires to you want to get from that?

___

Now that you have completed 3 cycles of this process, I invite you to simply feel where you are at. Take a few minutes, to write about your thoughts and feelings about where you have ended up. If you feel like there I still something deeper, keep repeating steps 1-3 (on a separate piece of paper) until you are where you want to be, then come back to this question.

___

Put Down the Book and DO Something!

My hope, is that this place of clarity and understanding about who you are, and what you really want in life. This IS your Diving Mission and purpose! Knowing this, can support you in so many ways as you move through your life. If you still feel like you aren't there, keep going. Stay in the discovery. Don't stop! Keep asking yourself to go deeper, and deeper. When you get it, you'll know it.

Extra credit: I have one final extra credit assignment. Very few people actually take me up on this one, however those who do, have had huge successes in their lives since completing this assignment. Now that you know your Divine Mission & Purpose, do the following:
- Journal about the following, for 20 minutes a day, for 1 week.
    - It's 10 years form now. What was the last ten years of your life like, having lived (and accomplished) your Divine Mission & Purpose
    - Write it as if you are writing a journal entry, looking back over the last 10 years.
    - Be as detailed as possible. What did you accomplish? What is your life like?
    - Start over every single day. Don't start where you left off. Start fresh every day for the entire week.
    - Be conscious of your limiting beliefs as you write. When they pop up, stop them, set them aside, and keep writing.

- After you have written for 7 days minimum (some do 10 days!), take the LAST day that you wrote, and do the following:
    - Video yourself reading what you wrote on your last day.
    - Play "epic music" in the background. (Yes, I'm serious.) IF you aren't sure what Epic music is, do a YouTube search for "epic music" there are several compilations there. Pick one, and have it playing in the background for your recording. Who doesn't want a soundtrack for their life?! My favorite piece of epic music for this, is a song called Awake, by Full Tilt.
    - Don't skip in the music. It has a VERY important purpose here!
    - This might feel silly. It's ok. Do it anyway!
    - Sharing your video with those who will dream with you and support your mission is strongly encouraged!
    - Watch this video any time you forget.

14 - 90 DAYS OF BREAKTHROUGH

Now that you have dome some amazing ground work, you are ready to take the next 90 days of your life and seriously Break through the limiting beliefs that have kept you from being the man or woman that you were Designed to become! You might have already experienced some awesome discovery and breakthrough. If so, AWESOME! As I stated in the beginning, ACTION is what creates change. This entire book, up to this point was to prepare you for what is coming next. My only request, is that you proceed fully conscious and aware. CHOOSE how this experience will unfold in your life! It is my experience and belief that true, lasting change comes after a minimum of 90 days of daily action. This chapter is just that.

Follow the instructions, and enjoy the journey!

Instructions:

- For the next 90 days, each morning, turn the next page, and do what it says to do.
- You can take 2 days off each week. Be very conscious about your days off. My recommendation is to decide your days off, before you look at the task. Don't let a task and the feelings associated with it, to be your reason for taking a day off.
- Before you go to bed each night, come back and write about your experience. How did it impact you? What did you learn? What came up while you were doing it, etc.
- Don't look ahead & don't skip pages. Let the element of surprise support you. If you look ahead you may make up all kinds of stuff about what's coming, and totally rob yourself of the opportunity of discovery.
- Trust the process. Don't pre-judge what the purpose of the tasks are. They are meant to be whatever they are for you.
- Be brave. Fears may come up. Limiting Beliefs will likely fly. This is by design. This is how you can get them in front of you and fly! You only need 20 second of insane courage, to get through anything! What you find on the other side is often life changing!
- Each day, write about your experience, what you learned, how you grew, what the task meant to you or stirred up in you.

- If at any time in this process, you find that something is triggered from your past, that brings up old wounds or trauma, stop, take a deep breath, and seek support. Find a friend, counselor, therapist, coach, etc. to help you uncover and heal the wounds. Protect yourself, and make wise choices. If you need to skip a task because it stirs something up for you, then skip it!
- If you have completed my 6 week BBT Bootcamp, beware... Some tasks may be the same, but there are several new ones too!
- HAVE FUN! Never forget - Suffering is optional!

1. Write your proclamation on your mirrors, and at least 10 other places where you will see it often!

2. List your top 2 limiting beliefs. List 10 things you can do for each one to prove them wrong. Number them 1.1, 1.2, 1.3 - 1.10, 2.1, 2.2, 2.3 - 2.10, etc. (Refer to page 70 for help)

3. Determine your top limiting belief, and then spend 20 minutes journaling about where it came from.

4. Make a list of at least 25 things that you LOVE to do, but haven't in a long time.

5. Journal for 20 minutes about the things that your limiting beliefs have cost you.

6. Today is Play day! Do something today that makes you feel playful and fun!

7. Say your proclamation to 10 people today.

8. Reach out to someone from your past who you have unfinished business with, that has been weighing on you. Make an effort to clear it up.

9. Reach out to 5 people in your life and tell them something amazing that you appreciate about them.

10. Write a letter to yourself, forgiving yourself for a mistake you have made in your past.

11. Go back and look at Task #2. Do Item 1.5 from your list that you created.

12. Tell a stranger something great about you!

13. Do one of the things on the list that you wrote in task #4.

14. Pick one word from your proclamation that challenges you today. Do 2 things today to bring more of that word into your life.

15. Go back and look at Task #2. Do Item 1.2 from your list that you created.

16. Write down 25 things that you are grateful for in your life.

17. Do something to spoil yourself today.

18. Go back and look at Task #2. Do Item 1.9 from your list that you created.

19. Ask 15 people in your life, to tell you 2 things they love the most about you! Write them all down.

20. Go back and look at Task #2. Do Item 1.10 from your list that you created.

21. Initiate a conversation with a stranger today. Find out something interesting about them.

22. Go back and look at Task #2. Do Item 1.1 from your list that you created.

23. Make a list of your top 25 greatest lifetime accomplishments.

24. Give 3 strangers genuine compliments today.

25. Who is one of the most important people in your life? Take 30 minutes and write as many things as you can think of that you are grateful for about them. Read it to them when you are finished.

26. Go back and look at Task #2. Do Item 1.6 from your list that you created.

27. Do one of the things on the list that you wrote in task #4.

28. Go back and look at Task #2. Do Item 2.9 from your list that you created.

29. Think of a person from your past that you need to forgive. Write them a letter, forgiving them. You don't have to send it to them, but you absolutely can, if you want!

30. Do one of the things on the list that you wrote in task #4.

31. Go back and look at Task #2. Do Item 2.2 from your list that you created.

32. Make a decision about something that will be different in your life in the next 30 days, and take action on ONE thing towards it.

_____
_____
_____
_____
_____
_____
_____
_____
_____
_____
_____
_____
_____
_____
_____
_____
_____
_____
_____
_____
_____
_____
_____
_____
_____
_____
_____
_____

33. Go back and look at Task #2. Do Item 1.7 from your list that you created.

34. Go back and look at Task #2. Do Item 2.7 from your list that you created.

35. Take yourself out on a date. Not just to a movie. On a real date!

36. Call 3 people you love and tell them something you love about them.

37. Write a letter to yourself, forgiving yourself for anything you view as a shortcoming or failure.

38. Go back and look at Task #2. Do Item 2.5 from your list that you created.

39. Write a letter to your 5 year old self. Talk about what you wish for him/her.

40. Go back and look at Task #2. Do Item 2.6 from your list that you created.

41. Play the conscious word game. Keep track in your phone or on a piece of paper. Every time a limiting thought comes to mind, make a mark. At the end of the day, notice how many marks you have.

42. Write a list of at least 50 things that are amazing about you!

43. Go back and look at Task #2. Do Item 2.4 from your list that you created.

44. Reach out to 5 people from your past that you have lost contact with.

45. Think of a person from your past that you need to ask for forgiveness. Write them a letter, asking them to forgive you. You don't have to send it to them, but you absolutely can, if you want!

46. Go back and look at Task #2. Do Item 2.1 from your list that you created.

47. Do one of the things on the list that you wrote in task #4.

48. BE your proclamation today in everything that you do.

49. Go back and look at Task #2. Do Item 2.3 from your list that you created.

50. Play the conscious word game. Keep track in your phone or on a piece of paper. Every time you say "but" "try" or "can't" make a mark. At the end of the day add them up. Donate $5 to the charity of your choice for each mark.

51. Go back and look at Task #2. Do Item 1.8 from your list that you created.

52. Decide which word in your proclamation is the most challenging for you. Do 3 things today that honor that word.

53. Go back and look at Task #2. Do Item 2.10 from your list that you created.

54. Go back and look at Task #2. Do Item 2.8 from your list that you created.

55. **Buy a helium balloon. Tie it to your wrist or waist, and wear it everywhere you go today. Have fun with it!** (If you need to postpone because of work limitations, I strongly suggest that you make this one up on a day that you can.)

56. Say your proclamation to 3 strangers today.

57. Do 5 random acts of kindness today! (5 random things for 5 random strangers)

58. Do something today that scares you.

59. Smile and say hello to 10 strangers today.

60. Today is silly day. Do something today that makes you feel silly.

61. Go back and look at Task #2. Do Item 1.3 from your list that you created.

62. What word in your proclamation is the most challenging today? Practice being THAT word.

63. Go back and look at Task #2. Do Item 1.4 from your list that you created.

64. Say your proclamation out loud, in a public place, with at least 5 strangers present.

Take 20 minutes, and write about your experience over the course of this chapter. How have you changed? What have you learned about yourself?

Put Down the Book and DO Something!

15 - THE DANDELION

Dandelions. The most misunderstood, mislabeled of all flowers. Proud homeowners spend hundreds of dollars to eradicate them, in order to have a "perfect" lawn! "Weeds!" they say! The whole attitude around dandelions confuses me! On one hand, they are said to be the scourge... the curse to pretty lawns everywhere... yet when they go to seed, we can blow on them and all of our wishes come true?! Huh?!?!

Then if we look at the nutritional content, Dandelion is a very rich source of beta-carotene which we convert into vitamin A. This flowering plant is also rich in vitamin C, fiber, potassium, iron, calcium, magnesium, zinc, and phosphorus. It's a good place to get B complex vitamins, trace minerals, organic sodium, and even some vitamin D too. The greens also contain vitamins C and B6, thiamin, riboflavin, calcium, iron (crucial for generating red blood cells), potassium (to help regulate heart rate and blood pressure), and manganese. Other nutrients present in dandelion greens include folate, magnesium, phosphorus, and copper.

My QUESTION is this: WHO SAID THEY ARE WEEDS?! Who told that lie, that we all believed?! Why did we believe it?

I hope you know I'm not talking about dandelions! Who said what lies about you? What lies in your head have you been believing? Hopefully, this process has helped you discover some of your value, your gold, your uniqueness. Hopefully, you have become aware how absolutely amazing, valuable, beautiful, and special you are! Like the dandelion, you are of Divinity! You have power that you may have ever known before!

My invitation to you is that you embrace this Divine truth! Embrace who you are! Embrace the power that you have within you to reach all of your dreams and goals!

You have only scratched the surface. Stay conscious! Don't go back to sleep! Take an opportunity EVERY DAY of your life to build more evidence of your greatness! Have fun, and enjoy your journey! Namaste.

Put Down the Book and DO Something!

ABOUT THE AUTHOR

Roger Webb has been a Life/Wellness Coach and Sales & Management trainer for individuals & companies all over the globe for over 20 years. He has worked with all levels of businesses, from small sales organizations to fortune 500 companies. As a Master NLP Practitioner, Roger has a keen insight to the subconscious mind, and has a deep commitment to helping others break through their limiting beliefs, to achieve amazing success, both personally and professionally.

Roger is a single father, and has raised 5 amazing kids on his own, and loves working with kids, fathers, and families. He is deeply committed to empowering others to live lives of passion, authenticity, optimal health, and love!

In mid 2013, Roger started a Network marketing venture, and within 2 years, he built an organization of over 2500 people extending around the globe. He is successfully supporting his team members in achieving goals and dreams they never thought possible!

You can learn more about Roger and the work he does, by visiting one of the following websites: bbtguru.com or rogerdoes.life

www.ingramcontent.com/pod-product-compliance
Lightning Source LLC
Chambersburg PA
CBHW071505040426
42444CB00008B/1508